Praise for *Miriam's Book*

From the very first line, "Before the night stoops like a widow over a field of bones," as Harold Schweizer's stunning poem sequence opens, we are in the presence of a great poet. At once metaphor of loss and grief and fractal of Europe's post-war landscape, *Miriam's Book* comprises a harrowing tale of the struggles of one young couple—the narrator's Jewish mother and gentile father—to survive the war. The text hovers among partial memories and shifting versions, and between an English made eloquent by distance and fragments of a German that, like Celan's, still bears the traces of the Nazis' horrific devastation. In the end, Schweizer bears compassionate witness to a truth, the soul's capacity to create out of trauma beauty, though it be harsh and fill us with awe and terror—which is to say, *Miriam's Book* unfolds in the terrain of the sublime.

—Cynthia Hogue, author of *Revenance* and *The Incognito Body*

Harold Schweizer's poetic novella *Miriam's Book* is literally the best reading that has come before me in several years—fiction or poetry.

The period is WWII and Miriam is Jewish, escaping Germany, eventually to Switzerland. Her lover is

Heinrich, who eventually is conscripted into Hitler's military. What befalls Miriam is nothing we would wish for anyone, but we don't find her pitiable because she is so appealing, courageous, and alive, taking her chances at life, at love, at surviving. Schweizer accomplishes the conveyance of this one soul with such grace we feel ourselves delivered as she meets and avoids discovery. The book reads like a mystery novel, and because of its filmic, piecemeal, disjunctive manner the reader stutters with its actions like the flickering of old films. The unsteadiness somehow carries us through even as it threatens to fail, omits things, leaps across gaps as its narrator, Stern Krebernick, leaves himself out, the inner ambush of his silence broken only by Miriam's scant address to him at the close.

When a story is so severe it would be unbefitting to heap praise in the usual way. Perhaps only through the tenacity of lovers can we be brought to bear the weight of this ever unknowable, unspeakable period. Through this book we experience how much it takes to persevere beyond basic needs, toward heart's core and even further: to enter the almost silent nucleus of one soul finding its way. *Miriam's Book* is a resonant cry that reverberates long after one has read it to the last.

—Tess Gallagher, author of *Midnight Lantern: New and Selected Poems* and *The Man from Kinvara: Short Stories*

In Harold Schweizer's strikingly innovative book-length poem *Miriam's Book*, time becomes part of an emotionally charged interior narration. Set in the turbulence of northern Europe as WWII unfolds, the book depicts a world in which a character might survive certain death but bear the marks of such a possible outcome as if what did not happen could be even more significant than what did. Schweizer's characters carry these projected narratives on their bodies like phantom limbs. These real pains from missing body parts and psychic losses merge and reverberate on another plane of reality which is already embedded in this one. *Miriam's Book* is a stunning achievement and may well prove to be one of the most accomplished prose poems of recent times.

—Charles Borkhuis, author of *Disappearing Acts* and *Afterimage*

MIRIAM'S BOOK:
A POEM

Harold Schweizer

Does it matter?

Fomite
Burlington, VT

ISBN-13: 978-1-942515-74-6

Library of Congress Control Number: 2016961834

Fomite
58 Peru Street
Burlington, VT 05401
www.fomitepress.com

Cover Art: Delia Bell Robinson
Cover Design:
Phoebe Schweizer West | www.phoebewest.com

For Saundra Kay

Write books only if you are going to say in them the things you would never dare confide to anyone.

E.M. Cioran

Contents

1 The Knife And Scissor Sharpener
Rides The Stone Wheel

Kriegszittern	3
Sounds	6
The Moon	8
Water	11
The Spoon	13
Bread	15
Blood	17

2 A Thing Testifies By Its Material Proximity
To The Human Body

Eyes	21
471325	22
The Foot	23
Cattle Car	26
Things	28
Numbers	30
Hands	32

3 They Fly In The Breath Of Living Things

Hands	37
Shadow	40

Wheels   43
The Star   45
Light   48
Breath   51
Schnittstellen   *52*
Blood   54

4   THE SUN'S ANEMIC SHEEN ON THE SNOW-
COVERED SLOPES OF THE GLARNER ALPS

The Speed of Falling   59
Ribbons   62
Hands   65
Night Sky   67
North Wind   69

5   A CLOWNISH TRIO OF SALTIMBANQUES
PIROUETTING ON THE HORIZON

Blood   73
Wheel   75
Scherenschnitt   *78*
Light   80
Earth   83

6   THE WATER NYMPHS COME OUT AND BATHE
IN THE MOONLIGHT

Snow   87

Die Moldau   91

Milk Light   94

Miriam Dreams and Does Not Remember
     Her Dream the Next Morning   96

Silent Night   97

Fastnacht   101

7   THE AIR A COLD SLAP THE SKY SLATE AND A LIGHT RAIN

Partisans   105

Bombs   108

Stecken   111

The Boat   114

Blood   117

Elijah   118

8   BIRDS LIKE SMALL DISHES RATTLING IN A CUPBOARD

Birthday   123

Apfelstrudel   126

Bird   128

Duden   130

Eat   132

Sleep   133

Acknowledgments   135

1

The Knife And Scissor Sharpener Rides The Stone Wheel

Kriegszittern[1]

Before the night stoops
like a widow over a field of bones. Heinrich
Krebernick under the Ferris wheel holds his arm out
in a right angle *Fräulein darf ich fragen* if she wants to
take a ride twigs breaking from her elbows. She looks
with eyes dark as falling shakes. Her head *nein danke*
then without speaking so much as a paragraph
between them facing each other pluck at a stick of
cotton candy. They part having hastily exchanged
their telephone numbers on slips of paper that

she folding and tearing on
the fold supplies 471325 and that each shyly clasps in
the dark of their respective pockets Heinrich on his
way writhes in his chest a flywheel in whose flight
Miriam plays the harmonica rising its wail in scattered
angles into the vast night approaching Berlin 1933 the
paper. With her number on it. Miriam with her hand
on Heinrich's number steps across her threshold like
the proverbial aspen leaf to ignite her gas

---

1 War tremors

3

stove. As if
choreographed by an intendant of a small chamber
play Heinrich's arm's gesture has lifted a curtain
under which they are to pass before the pale
beginnings of the new day but tonight she unfolds

a small bird and flattens
the wing with her fingers pats it down on a prominent
surface say on the chest of drawers here with the
black marble top and looks up at the falling of all
things born like paper. *Unter den Linden* file the
brown-shirted *Sturmgeziefer* the Chancellor waves

Heinrich's arm angled one
hundred five degrees ($105°$) the carnival workers
dismantle the rides Miriam bends over Heinrich's slip
of paper that has partially refolded itself during the
night and flies a small wing on the marble top she
jerks the paper with her thumb and combs it sideways
with her fore and middle fingers. With her right hand
she combs her hair in the mirror over the chest

of drawers Heinrich to the
northwest approximately three kilometers away but
what are numbers at his table eating an egg and a
piece of rye bread thinly buttered holds her slip
before him considering it. Miriam with her comb in
her hand says *nu Heinrich* while the carnival workers

tie their clatter to the side of their wagons. Blue irises six of them are carried into a room and placed in a high tubular glass onto the doily on a small wooden table. Miriam paces in front of her window the glass covered roofs of the *Anhalter Bahnhof* with its nine arches and twin corner towers six blue irises. When she turns

her head a glass peal of light sounds a thin blade of white from the station. In the quiver of her fingers she has woven the small slip of paper through the comb's teeth. Had she known that she carried in her weaving prophecies in which she could have read her future if she could have read the teeth of her comb she would have known she was the carrier of the star on which her number would be woven on the shores of the *Wannsee*. The comb shakes

in her hand and the paper in the comb and the number on the paper. Heinrich does not know her finger trembles on his fate and he does not in the nature of human propensities to shrug off intimations of astral destinations have an inkling that their numbers so to speak had been called.

Sounds

Their numbers so to
speak had been called. My harmonica steadies my
hands. Better if I play *ombra mai fu* on the zither look
a little night

(Berlin 1926)

rain has fallen she runs
her finger on the wet window sill 471325 471325
471325 471325 flies down a flight of stairs lifts the
heavy black receiver off its silvery hook her eyelids
flutter too late Bb Bb Bb. But less than an hour
471325 471325 and she hears *hallo hier ist Heinrich*

Krebernick my hands. *Stein ja bitte* I cannot quiet my
hands. He jumps onto his Excelsior rehearses his lines
rests

                                his eyes on the nape of
her neck and the seams of her silk stockings his hands
sleeping songbirds on the handlebars pedals up
Charlottenburger Chaussee. The carnival workers'
gaily painted trailers their carousel horses their
monkey cages their small trucks their food carts their
mobile repair kits their movable school trailer with
its bell flow a red and white band of streamers down
Charlottenburger Chaussee turning into Grosser
Stern while she waits in *Tiergarten* near the river
Spree. A knife and scissor sharpener

                                lifts the back of his bicycle
on its stand turns the saddle to the back climbs it and
rides the writhing stone wheel of the *Reichs* racket to
the sound of metal. While Heinrich in a sheath of light
under the linden trees about to turn into Spreeallee.
Runs into the drums and trumpets of a column of the
brown-shirted *Sturmgeziefer* and the vaudeville
monkeys' *zum Hitlergruss* right monkey arms aloft *die
Strasse frei den braunen Batallionen.*[2]

---

2 Lines from the popular "*Horst Wessel Lied*," "the street free for the
brown battalions"

The Moon

Die Strasse frei den
braunen Batallionen. In her quivering hands time is
bent. Miriam in the comb's teeth singing stones that
have been given a voice. Her skirt gets caught in the
spokes of her bicycle's back wheel Heinrich trying to
disentangle it tears it and Miriam not given to laughter
laughs they do not know that at that moment

they are Jacob and Rachel
standing in a vast wheat field dotted with the red of
poppies albeit with two bicycles at the point where
the horizon rears up into the blue of the June sky and
the air is fragrant with the scent of grass and wheat
and the slightly acid smell of pine. And Jacob holds
Rachel awkwardly across the frame of her bicycle she
flails in the knife and scissor sharpener's wheel I play

my zither mostly she says
pushing him weakly away to steady my hands my
hands are birds startled by a sudden noise say of a
knock on the door one will not have expected so late
at night and of a sudden cacophony of voices and the

barking of dogs *schneller schneller* dressing what one
can find and the hasty packing of suitcases and the
doily the family menorah whittled of rosewood the
harmonica the zither under my arm perhaps a little

brother who will not find
his shoes and who will walk barefoot hold my hand all
the way to the train station and the voices and the
barking and the zither under my arm and the quieting
of the children all will be as one says without knowing
better well but the terrible tearing and lunging to the
right the left. Are we still

speaking of the birds that
fly where Miriam's hands fly without knowing their
destinations about her in sharp circles and sudden
plungings but the zither's flat board calls her hands
from their prophetic vertical risings to a solemn
horizontal gliding and stroking over the thirty-five
strings on which she plays for Heinrich Händel's *Largo*
crying it? He stands mute as the block of rosewood
before the menorah was whittled out of it. Smoking
but she knows about the necessary mutualities of
beauty and loss to sense what he means in his wooden
silence since she too cannot say what it is she knows
though *es ist ihr auf den Leib geschrieben* it is written
on her body and lets her birds do as it were the talking.
She lifts her torn

skirt off the rack and
fender and stands to contemplate the oil-streaked
tears in the fabric which ruin on the scale of things
will be laughable. It is four o'clock and the moon
hangs in a pale white. Wisp of a sickle whose outer
circumference is sharply white in the light blue sky.
The sounds of shrieking children from the nearby
Strandbad are the same all over the world. That
night

Miriam's hands lie in an
ecstatic stillness on the covers of her bed while the
moon spells the contours of the letter *z* which is the
letter to initiate the word *zunehmend* and whose
tiny compared to the size of the moon concave half-
circle upper part open to the left stands for the *waxing*
moon while the *waning* moon is assigned the convex
letter *a* for *abnehmend* and which coincidence
between human and heavenly things always seems to
Miriam who monthly witnesses it in her body to imply
an incomprehensible harmony of all things between
heaven and earth this month she is late.

Water

Between heaven and
earth this month she is late. Heinrich's bicycle leans
against the wooden fence of the *Wannsee
Strandbad*.[3] The windless day has laid glass on the
water. The monkeys are slain.[4] They walk away
pushing their bicycles her hand in her hair where she
might finger a sudden trigger that would open a gate
through which they could enter under old trees and
find a dappled clearing with a cloth already spread out
and bread and wine and water and the sounds of
songbirds and insects humming in the hot summer air
but she removes. Her hand and reaches it across vast
golden fields and a thousand red poppies towards
Heinrich who has no gate to open. The needle

with which she tries to
mend her skirt that night stutters through the fabric in
the form of a 6 the point of the intersection of the

---

3 The Wannsee lido was closed to Jews in 1934.
4 Vaudeville artists had taught their monkeys the Hitler salute.
Consequently, the monkeys were ordered to be killed.

lines being the horizontal cloth spread over her hips
the wheat field meeting the sky over her empty lap
where she keeps a secret she does not know how to
please or silence 471325. She flies down the flight of
471325 stairs *Miriam Stein nu ja schön am Samstag
danke* on Saturday thank you.

Her room on the second
floor on Alte Jakobsstrasse looks out onto a tree in
which at certain evening hours sudden flocks of
finches used to gather in loud rattling riot before they
would all at once as if a conductor had given a sign
with his baton quiet for the night. The traffic outside
her open window heaves in the rhythm of her 6 and
though she is on the verge of ceasing to breathe
as she sews the cloth she breathes and weaves her
needle's number in her downward leaning face as if
she would once her sewing has ended permit herself
to fall into the sky that the windless air has opened
underneath her in the water.

The Spoon

The sky that the windless
air has opened underneath her in the water Miriam
waits on Saturday returns on Sunday waits more
deeply and once more while Heinrich's body swings in
the Spree bedded in the leaves shingled by the calm
current waits and the day feeds on its own body eats
itself backwards from its hind legs. Her eyelids flutter
like moths in her hands his number. The oil stain has
not come out all the stitching in vain this month she
thinks she is late. Miriam's head is bent

to her mother during the
last weeks of her rheumatic inflammations in the
afternoon light in whose almost horizontal slant tiny
dust particles float she folds the towel under her chin
and lifts her face towards the spoon and in the
concave reflection of the spoon's inner curve after it
has left her mother's mouth Miriam sees herself
hanging inverted in a room whose ceiling

is down and whose floor
up and the table the bed with her mother in it and the

nightstand with the washbasin and the water in it hang suspended down from the floor.

Bread

And the nightstand with
the washbasin and the water in it hang suspended
down from the floor. She forgets to wind up her clock
and oversleeps by almost forty minutes late to work
flies down her flight of stairs runs across Alte
Jackobsstrasse to the bakery just five minutes across
Franz-Künstler Strasse weaving as she runs with her
forefinger in her skirt pocket the number 6 as if her
finger were a needle withdraws her hand to press the
massive metal door handle hears the familiar ring
Frau Heimbacher eyes swollen red waves her frantically
to the back of the store behind the counter takes her
hand leads her past

the ovens to the back
door and thrusts Miriam a pounder of *Dunkelbrot die
warn hier* they were here look. What they did to the
Fröhlichs' *Metzgerei* lucky you are late today what a
day! *Wir dürfen den Juden kein Brot mehr verkaufen*
we are no longer allowed to sell bread to Jews *schon
gar keine* let alone employ one as *Verkäuferin*. Miriam
mute

as a cry in a stone.
Clutches the loaf runs back across Franz-Künstler
Strasse and along Alte Jackobsstrasse up the flight of
stairs to her room where she says *Heinrich*.
Motionless under the Ferris wheel *Heinrich Heinrich*
when I need you until she hears Herr Pfenniger the
Hauswart [5] downstairs lock the front door. Miriam
eats a piece of *Dunkelbrot* in the twilight of her room
with a plate of cauliflower

                                  she has made the day
before her eyes dark as falling. Large flocks of
migratory birds gather in long twittering rows on
wires and in trees like small dishes rattling in a
cupboard and a cold rain. Falls and the days shorten
Miriam on a yellow bench [6] in *Tiergarten* trying to
smooth the creases out of the paper presses it onto a
wooden slat and runs her finger down the paper's
length.

---

5 A concierge who cleans the staircase in an apartment building for
a slight reduction in rent
6 Jews were allowed to sit only on designated yellow benches in
Berlin.

Blood

And runs her finger down
the paper's length on platform 4 *Anhalter Bahnhof* her
hand on the handle of the suitcase the other hand on
the handle of the zither case she puts them down.
Flies circles in her handbag the ticket she can feel it
holds it with her hand plunged in the darkness
waiting this train does not have a car designated for
Jews she must wait for another one and spends the
night her head on her suitcase in the crowded
Wartesaal für Juden the next morning she sits on her
way to Nuremberg in the corridor on her suitcase the
zither case on her knees her handbag around her neck
3. Klasse nur für Juden seething. She bleeds on her
skirt I am not born when she returns her zither case.
Is gone

in Nuremberg she buys
an apple *Judendreck* is accused of stealing it sleeps on
her suitcase her ticket in her hand her hand in her
purse finds a window seat on the next train two days
later and sits in a steady tremor. She arrives in
Feldkirch works in the *Bäckerei* Knell her aunt's

bakery has her name changed to Herlinde Jung and her new passport without the ꗧ though she secretly keeps it in her new name is the handiwork of a Jesuit priest beheaded in the Munich Stadelheim Prison for high treason on 2 April 1945.

2

A Thing Testifies By Its Material Proximity To The Human Body

Eyes

1675 days before the
beheading Miriam kneads and molds her tremor into
bread on a small wooden table in the *Backstube*
because her trembling made her spill the change and
the war. Breaks out she is conscripted to work as
a nurse in the *Reservelazarett 1 Antoniushaus* nor can
she bind wounds any better than she could wrap
loaves of *Dunkelbrot* that do not bleed. Among
stumps upper jaws a stream of mucus paper bandages
she smokes her *Stellas* and extinguishes the match by
jerking her hand violently from left to right as if all the
smoothing of Heinrich's number could be done by

the armless *Untergeziefer*
Detlev Knebbel who one late afternoon after she has
emptied his cup of mucus and bends over his face
bandaged like a loaf of bread raises his stumps and
shouts **Hitler gib mir meine Augen zurück**[7] while
his glistening mucus slithers slowly down the drain.

---

7 Hitler, give me back my eyes.

471325

While his glistening
mucus slithers slowly down the drain *Untergeziefer*
Knebbel rears up is held down by *Schwester* Herlinde
sh-sh-sh-sh she whispers to his bandaged head softly
sings *heile heile säge* he calms if it hadn't been for that
slip of paper with Pfenniger's 471325 on it I still know
it by heart I forgot it in my pocket back in Berlin you
know I would have been promoted and never lost he
lifts his body onto his upper arms his head slightly
cocked to the side that's my number she whispers

my arms and eyes I would
have been promoted to *Hauptgeziefer* your number?
Where is Heinrich? She holds him by his shoulders
where is Heinrich? What happened to

your number? He sinks
into his bed you are his *Schätzle*? With the flowers?
Yes she cries dead.

The Foot

The flowers? Yes she cries
dead. On 1 October 1943 because the red cross on the
roof has been over painted? We don't know it is a
beautiful almost cloudless day 12:34 15 flying
fortresses of the allied forces drop 36 bombs 500 kilos
each onto Tisis and Tosters one into the middle of the
Antoniushaus where Miriam whose name is Herlinde
with the secret ℈ has been told to seek cover in the
Stiegenhaus the staircase hears plain and clear the
screaming of the bomb that falls

on her she floats with
Heinrich in the calm current of the Spree with the
shingled leaves at the bottom her ears are water
where she holds him under wood plaster stone dust in
a dark airless cavity in the center of Europe climb
down pull *reisst mir den Fuss nicht ab* don't rip off my
foot she cries drinks water they reach down to her try.
To lift the block of concrete with iron poles she who
was lithe and light-footed flew down her staircase in
Berlin they cannot reach her in the narrow cavity
reisst mir den Fuss nicht ab they pull her by her arms
once more morphine she drifts into a night taller than
the Ferris wheel a small knife a hand-

saw the kind one uses for
delicate metal work. Karl Schreber who works in the
Spinnerei [8] ties a rubber band tightly around her calf
under the knee runs the knife like a red ankle bracelet
around her lower leg cuts skin and flesh as instructed
by Dr. Knuthman who leans over the cavity about five
centimeters (5 cm) above the ankle and saws the

fibula first then the tibia
as instructed by Dr. Knuthman asks for garden
shears stretching his right arm out the hole without
turning his head to cut the Achilles tendon which

---

8 Textile factory

slips back and forth under the saw without tearing
Herlinde. Awakens on 3 October

                                        on 8 October the black
roots of Miriam's hair show against the white
pillowcase like commas in an unwritten book.

Cattle Car

Like commas in an
unwritten book the nurses report to Dr. Knuthman Dr.
Knuthman reports to the authorities two young SS
Geziefer smartly arrive in elegant black uniforms
boots heel click right arm one hundred five
degrees (105°) *Heilittla* Dr. Knuthman *Heilittla* the
nurses *Heilittla* make Miriam stand up she faints is
promptly taken to the *Justizanstalt* [9] where Herman
and Elfriede Knell are already waiting Karl Schreber is
arrested in the *Spinnerei* all three are hanged that
afternoon in the *Spazierhof* [10] while Miriam awaits a
transport for Theresienstadt via Innsbruck where she
is heaved footless into a cattle car on a long train of
cattle cars that has crossed the Brenner from Italy and
dies less than an hour into the ride or

she dies in a small room
overlooking the pretty village square in
Theresienstadt at sunset say or shortly after arriving

---

9 Courthouse and prison
10 Inner court of the *Justizanstalt*, literally "court of strolling,"
where many executions were held until 1947

on the long Birkenau platform where she hardly has
to walk or be carried more than a few hundred steps
to the gas chambers under the slack sky.

Things

A few hundred steps to
the gas chambers under the slack sky or Miriam is
sent to a Prague hospital from Theresienstadt or from
Auschwitz to a Krakow hospital in either of which it
doesn't matter because these are universals she
empties:

Urine bottles glasses
with phlegm pots with feces buckets with bloodied rags
baskets with miscellaneous surgical articles rubber
bands clamps pins needles pads bandages and small
body parts teeth jaws eyes ears fingers flaps of skin
penises hands feet bones all of which she piles onto a
trolley and carts to the *Krematorium*. As she loads
and discards their sudden silent

thingness they have in
the way a thing testifies by its material proximity to the
human body borne witness to an unspeakable
suffering in which Miriam herself partakes and for
which reason though no earthly inhabitant would

understand it she is chosen who knows by whom to
live as silently

as a thing in Prague or
perhaps in Krakow. Though she can be heard loudly
rattling her various containers down the rows of beds
above all she can be heard rocking from wooden foot.
To foot so that her footless leg bears the weight of her
body but briefly in a sharp staccato **pit** followed by
her left foot's slapping **pat** while at the same time
causing Miriam's hips pivoting on her prosthetic foot
to turn slightly leftward. She never falls except
shortly after the amputation when she forgets getting
up at night that she has no right foot although she
feels it most days twisting and thrashing on her leg as
if the foot wanted to bend grotesquely upwards to

touch her kneecap. Prague
or Krakow suffering is endured neither in latitudes
nor longitudes but in sublimely varied permutations
of intimate material proximities mostly of inhuman
things with human bodies which in Miriam's case is
the conjunction of her stump with the padding in the
prosthetic socket. The tight fitting the swelling the
chafing the bleeding the sweating the small sharp
invisible fold in the padding of the prosthetic socket
are multiplied in each step she takes though the sum
of her suffering never amounts to a number.

Numbers

The sum of her suffering
never amounts to a number or to such numbers as the
number of the dead (210) on 1 October 1943 who
no longer suffer or the 110 injured who suffer or the 35
bombs and the 500 kilo weight of each of them and
the damage they make count as we may. Count as we
may pairs of eyes ears arms legs feet hands kidneys
ovaries lungs testicles breasts two brain sides two
chambers. Of the heart we inexplicably have two (2)
of each but for many among the wounded that is not
enough which is perhaps blasphemy. Steps are
countable and the body's pressure

in the prosthetic socket is
measurable as kilograms multiplied by square
centimeters (kg x cm^2) even if one seeks to relieve the
weight as quickly as possible and one can no doubt
put a finger on the numbers themselves but what are
numbers as one can on the frequency curve either of
Miriam's trembling twigs breaking from her elbows or
as one can put a finger as it were on the slow and
solemn cosine curve (approx. y=10 cos 3x) of

Heinrich's swinging in the Spree with the shingled
leaves at the bottom

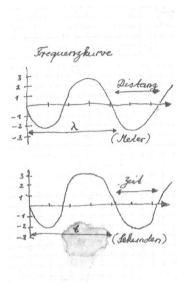

had he ever been found
or for that matter on the quantity theoretically of
the moisture excreted by Karl Schreber hanging
blindfolded in the *Spazierhof* and who must have
thought briefly he was to receive an *Auszeichnung.*[11]

---

11 Medal

Hands

And who must have
thought briefly he was to receive an *Auszeichnung*
while all that is measured out in indifferent numbers
falling from the sky or in pressure points in the
darkness of the body's intimacies suffering has in
common with goodness both being secret antidotes to
numbers and dates in that both are unaccountable

both groundless as a
staircase while the bombs fall though one is common
and the other rare as miracles. For what if the nurses
do not report Miriam and neither does Dr. Knuthman?
To add miracle to miracle and she were to end up
wrapping bouillon cubes hunched over an assembly
line at the Maggi soup factory in Kemptthal
Switzerland? We can no more account for it than for
her lost foot. Her hair

is black she smokes her
Stellas and relieves her twitching with disproportional
jerkings of her arms when she extinguishes the match.
She has bought herself a used zither from a music

shop in Marktgasse 47 Winterthur where she rents a
room in the evening she sits by the weak light of her
window and thinks whose hands are these on my
zither the one on the left half opened as if it wanted to
take flight in a fluttering the one on the right holding
itself like a stone? On Monday she is moved to the

vegetable processing section at *Maggi Suppen* because
of her trembling she can be seen the third

                              from left in this
picture with her head bent slightly forward seated
on a stool nine hours a day with a free Saturday
afternoon which Jules Maggi was the first to
initiate in Switzerland the cauliflower in her
lap. Where she keeps

Heinrich's secret that
on more than one occasion she has to be determined
to keep and is called *Judenkrüppel* by one of her
jilted claimers though how she gets to wrap bouillon
cubes and cut cauliflower in Kemptthal remains to
be seen.

3

They Fly In The Breath Of Living Things

Hands

How she gets to wrap
bouillon cubes and cut cauliflower in Kemptthal
remains to be seen for Heinrich's hands are dreaming
on the handlebars the nape of her neck the soft curve
of her hips. He hardly hears the brown-shirted
Sturmgeziefer drumming. The monkeys raise their
right monkey arms (105°) *zum Hitlergruss* the small
crowd gathered to watch the carnival's farewell
parade roars the drumming

stops. The brown-shirted
Sturmgeziefer drag the vaudeville artist from his
monkey wagon beat him blue and bloody while
Heinrich already having turned into Spreeallee his
hands sleeping songbirds. Heinrich wake up your
songbirds lift them *mein Gott zum Hitlergruss* but
Heinrich. For which he will be apprehended near the
Spree his Excelsior flung to the ground *Papiere* papers
he reaches into his pocket his identity card her
471325 falls out flutters into the shade of a mulberry
bush where *Obergeziefer* Detlev Knebbel picks it up
aha! A telephone number and is walked

to the end of his life at the
end of Spreeallee they find his KPD [12] pin his thoughts
already weightless as his body in water but he ends up
in the narrow courts of Plötzensee Prison in Berlin
where he stands with a Jesuit Priest to be beheaded in
Stadelheim Prison in Munich where he stands
with Karl Schreber hanged in the sunlit *Spazierhof* of
the *Justizanstalt* where he stands in Deutschland with
all who hear the sound

of metal on the knife and
scissor sharpener's writhing stone wheel and is sent
to Columbia Concentration Camp in the Tempelhof
area he sits his legs strapped to the legs. Of the chair
and his hands in metal braces on the metal surface of
the table for 18 hours and a half the name of the
Fräulein bitte for whom the flowers

were intended. On
Wednesday exactly five days and 18 hours later
Obergeziefer Detlev Knebbel feels in his pocket a slip
of paper *mein Gott* the slip of paper 471325 471325
471325 471325 for which he will be demoted
abgereist says Herr Pfenniger on the other end
yesterday morning *mit Koffer und Zither wohin weiss*

---

12 Communist Party of Germany

ich nicht departed with suitcase and zither where I
don't know after 18 hours on the chair his fingernails
pulled Heinrich Krebernick whispers *ja Miriam Stein*
then soon to be

Untergeziefer Knebbel
slams the broad side of a hammer onto Heinrich's
hands and he is thrown into a small cell designed for a
single occupant and on occasion inhabited by up to
five prisoners during his incarceration his fingerbones.
Mend stiffly like the crooked prongs of a small garden
hoe. He will have to tell Miriam he can't keep the
appointment that Saturday he will come on Sunday

if we could have changed
the small head of a pin. Perhaps some October
morning let us say three years later in 1936. When
out of his narrow window he will catch sight of
swallows gathering like musical notes on the wires
high above the prison court though he will have lost
the count of days and weeks he will be shipped to
Sachsenhausen where he learns the Sachsenhausen
salute [13] to know what it means to refuse the Nazi
salute.

---

13 Prisoners were forced to squat with their arms outstretched in
front.

Shadow

He learns the Sachsen-
hausen salute to know what it means to refuse the
Nazi salute. If we could have changed the small head
of a pin with its red yellow hammer and sickle
covering a mere five square millimeters (5 mm^2) say if
we had inconvenienced a Jesuit priest to alter it to a
swastika while Heinrich turns into Spreeallee
forgetting the *Hitlergruss* because his hands are
dreaming songbirds on the handlebars he would have
shown his papers those also altered the flowers are
for my fiancée six irises Miriam Stein
Nationalsozialist! Heilittla. Aber eine Jüdin? But
since they have already been carried into a room and
put on a doily in a tubular vase on a small wooden
table and there is commotion and yelling coming from
the monkey trailer he is boot click click *Heilittla* let

go and finds himself next
to Miriam on a yellow bench and cannot explain his
whereabouts in 1933. Why it is he says that we want
to hide in the shadow of God's wings could one ever
be found there by anyone perhaps not

even by God himself
and surely one's hiding would be like a death to all others
that is why he says he has come a day late but he has
not come nor will he come for eleven years. Neither
could a Jesuit priest be found while Heinrich sits
stands or lies in that order mostly in cell no. 319 but
sometimes three doors down in no. 325 or across the
hall in no. 322 but what are numbers is shipped as we
have said to serve out his six-year sentence in
Sachsenhausen to know what it means to refuse the
Nazi salute and thereafter will but only if properly
reformed serve his *Vaterland* in the *Wehrmacht*
perhaps the Eastern Front. Miriam on a yellow bench
pulls out his number

© Yad Vashem

on the slip shaking in her
hand it rings. At Flensburgerstrasse 5 but no one
answers for eleven years and she reads his number
aloud so she might hear in her voice the shadow of
God's wings.

Wheels

So she might hear in her
voice the shadow of God's wings her eyes dark as
falling or if to counter such falling:

The mere movement of
Heinrich's arm raised slightly over his head angled
about one hundred five degrees (105°) would
have sufficed because it would have drawn precisely
no one's attention to the bicyclist with his front basket
filled with six irises who would have already turned
the corner of Spreeallee steering deftly with his left
hand and passing another smaller group of brown-
shirts right arm at 105° *Heilittla* and pedals up
towards the Spree with the shingled leaves at the
bottom leans his bicycle against the yellow bench six
irises and if the Ferris wheel

had kept turning and we
would have lost sight of them because the renegade
Krebernicks shy newlyweds would have been hiding
in attics cellars closets haylofts ditches pits forests
stairwells abandoned factories beds of trucks by the

cunning of helpers by the conscience of priests but it
is the knife and scissor sharpener's writhing stone
wheel not the Ferris wheel that is turning and no
hiding place can be dark enough in Deutschland for an
Israel Heinrich Krebernick a Jew decreed by marriage
and for a woman with a name like Miriam Stein who
for all we know ends up rolling a trolley with surgical
waste through the halls of U Nemocnice 2, 128
Hospital in Prague.

The Star

Who for all we know ends
up rolling a trolley with surgical waste through the
halls of U Nemocnice 2, 128 Hospital in Prague while
Heinrich having excelled in his reformation of the
German occupying force comfortably stationed in
Prague supervises in a camouflaged warehouse a
satellite of the Škoda Works in Pilsen the assembly of
artillery shells the same that are used in the offensive
in the Ardennes where he having been transferred
ausdrücklich als Kanonenfutter explicitly as cannon
fodder for an infraction against the racial purity law
the night of 11 February 1944 in a house at Katerinska
15 would have

defying his superiors died
of pneumonia. But Katerinska 15 is not far from
where Miriam leaves the hospital at half past six in the
evening six days a week pulling the iron gate to close
behind her with a double click and walks slowly eyes
down

down Lipova her cane

clicking on the cobbles where she rents a small room with a window with no tree in front and no birds like small dishes rattling in a cupboard her hands having to do all the flying and where in the twilight evenings she plays a rented zither to quiet her birds. While he seeking shelter from the light February drizzle in Betlémské Námésti tries the handle of the Betlémské Kapel door finds it open because it is Catholic and slips inside while Miriam's yellow star hovering approximately 150 centimeters above street level in the staccato rhythm of her cane that same Sunday evening crosses Betlémské Námésti and disappears in an adjoining alley. Or because Betlémské Kapel is Reformed since one ought to look for God not only in churches. Heinrich finds the door locked while Miriam's yellow star hovering approximately 150 centimeters above street level in the staccato rhythm of her cane that same evening across Betlémské Námésti catches

Heinrich's eye who stands smoking with his back to the church door trying to find shelter from the drizzle she. Sees him at the same time and emits a sharp

hardly muted cry her hand flutters to her mouth drops her cane she would have fallen had he not casting his eyes around the

square where 100 windows could have reported and
sentenced an *Untergeziefer* of the *Deutsche
Wehrmacht* holding a Jewish cripple to death.

Light

An *Untergeziefer* of the
Deutsche Wehrmacht holding a Jewish cripple to
death. He has pulled her into the adjoining alley into
which she had disappeared in our former permutation
under a small dark graveled partly covered gap
between the church and the next house she hangs in
his arms the weight of all the body parts she has
carted to the *Krematorium* but the shadow of God's
wings is a cold drizzle in which one can hide only
briefly. Miriam he says.

My foot she says *nu* is
abgerissen here and leads his hand below her knee
where he can feel the cold. Rounded surface of the
prosthetic socket she feels a fire rise into her face she
has let this man's hand touch her there better

they tear themselves.
Apart now each walk into his and her separate
directions on this night of 11 February in Prague back
to the relative safety of their *Reichs* assignments but
they condemn themselves to death. Miriam bending

her leg at the knee. So that Heinrich can hold her stump in his hands through the night at Katerinska 15 and in this holding a mitzvah is done not because one knows one has to do it but because one does it without knowing it though the night writhe in the stone wheel. In the invisible space between his crooked fingers and the small folds of skin over the bone if I were born by these hands

                      a space opens vast as light into which Rilke's flowers open and in which all that falls and cannot be mended is briefly repaired: a mother comes to her son holds his face in both her hands and gives him back his lips *Untergeziefer* Detlev Knebbel is given back his eyes even his hands though he didn't ask for them Heinrich Krebernick rises from the Spree with the shingled leaves at the bottom and survives three years in the Columbia Concentration Camp in the Tempelhof area where his fingers are wrapped in ribbons of sky and three years in the Sachsenhausen Concentration Camp where he learns the Sachsenhausen salute to know what it means to refuse the Nazi salute and Miriam is spared deportation and death we don't know why and wakes up the next morning her foot restored to her leg

                    a father unties his daughters from their grave in the ruins of the

Fröhlich's *Metzgerei* in Berlin and teaches them the
first principle of the weight of angels from the Book of
Proverbs they are light.

Breath

The weight of angels from
the book of proverbs they are light he says lifting his
finger there is no space not filled with them if you
carry them in a bowl to cool a child's fever they spill
over the sides like water they fly in the breath of living
things he puts his finger to his lips they are the breath
through which they fly they have no wings they are air.
No Sarah

born in your breath the
air you breathe is the bowl of light that you my
daughters Sarah Rebecka Ruth carry through your life
in each of your breaths is an angel's wing sheer as the
wings of dragonflies when they look.

They have wings? Let
your father speak Sarah when they look at you their
gaze is light he puts his finger to his lips as willow
dust they have their being in the air that lifts the
weight of flowers in the morning Frau Brodt enters
the room.

Schnittstellen

In the morning Frau Brodt
enters the room without knocking. Assuming rightly
because he left at half past seven Herr *Untergeziefer*
Krebernick is at work and since the number of
𝕾𝖈𝖍𝖓𝖎𝖙𝖙𝖘𝖙𝖊𝖑𝖑𝖊𝖓 [14] by which inhuman things can
penetrate the human body are infinite. How many

potential 𝕾𝖈𝖍𝖓𝖎𝖙𝖙𝖘𝖙𝖊𝖑𝖑𝖊𝖓 for
example are there say on the thirty-five centimeter
(35 cm) vertical seam of Miriam's silk stocking into
which she once had inserted a lower leg where a knife
a saw and a pair of garden shears could have found
countless iterations of penetration? It is not so
different in the case of a room on Katerinska 15 whose
door represents one millimeter (1 mm) on the silk
seam by which human suffering comes about. Miriam
reaching for her prosthetic foot. Other 𝕾𝖈𝖍𝖓𝖎𝖙𝖙𝖘𝖙𝖊𝖑𝖑𝖊𝖓
on the default graph we are using:

✻ 𝕹𝖔. 1 𝖙𝖍𝖊 𝖌𝖊𝖓𝖊𝖗𝖆𝖑 𝖕𝖗𝖔𝖕𝖊𝖓𝖘𝖎𝖙𝖞 𝖔𝖋 𝖑𝖆𝖓𝖉𝖑𝖔𝖗𝖉𝖘 𝖙𝖔 𝖌𝖔𝖘𝖘𝖎𝖕

---

14 Incision points

⸏ No. 2 the Gründlichkeit [15] by which the blackbooted Schutzgeziefer comb through Prague to find the escaped Jewish hospital employee

⸏ No. 3 the euphemisms by which slaves who do not show up for work on the morning of 12 february are called escaped employees

⸏ No. 4 the simple inability to sustain the secrecy of a cohabitation in a crowded city

⸏ No. 5 the banality of the chain breaking in the toilet tank that prevents Miriam from flushing the blood by which she monthly seals the harmony between heavenly and earthly things

⸏ No. 6 her nightmare of the bombing of Reservelazarett 1 Antoniushaus reisst mir den fuss nicht ab by which she wakes up the whole house

even as Heinrich's uniform solicits some respect though no doubt also a good deal of hatred so that no one would suspect *Untergeziefer* Krebernick to cohabit with *Ungeziefer*.[16] But since we know of the discovery of his *Rassenschande* [17] we must let Frau Brodt do her duty.

---

15 Meticulous care
16 Vermin
17 Racial impurity, literally racial shame, or racial defilement, enacted by the Reichstag on Sept. 15, 1935.

Blood

We must let Frau Brodt
do her duty close the door her hand on her mouth let
her walk down the stairs to the telephone next to the
cellar stairs because the wiring runs through the cellar
lift the black receiver off its silvery hook and make her
telephone call to inform some *Reichs* office charged
with the apprehension of fugitives traitors Jews
gypsies homosexuals and other criminals who will
dispatch a truckload of armed SS to arrest Miriam and
another truckload to do the same at Heinrich's
camouflaged warehouse where he is taking his nine
o'clock break eating bread and *Leberwurst.* But Frau
Brodt having it appears unwittingly

exposed herself to a gaze
light as willow dust as one might do without knowing
it when she stood in front of the telephone and does
not make the call for which she will contract
Heinrich's pneumonia and die. Climbs the stairs
carrying in her hands a bowl of light softly knocks
(this time)

on the door enters and
sits without invitation assuming a sudden intimacy it
is perhaps the intimacy of conspirators of which
Miriam has unexpectedly become one while she
shaking fails to tighten the strap over the knee
whereof Frau Brodt inquires in whispering
handwringing but above all if the man who wears a
Deutsche uniform a small percentage of whose body
warmth

might still be detectable
under the covers wears it she hopes only to keep off
the cold. And who will learn at half past five that same
12th of February that though Heinrich and Miriam
have been found they are found hidden if briefly in the
shadow of God's wings. Meanwhile *Untergeziefer*
Albert Friedrich

who has unsuspectingly
passed merely twenty times the anniversary of his
death which is to be this very day at a quarter to six
waits for *Untergeziefer* Krebernick in Frau Brodt's
living room although he has orders to take the files by
bicycle to the camouflaged warehouse but decides
lazily because of the cold February drizzle to drop
them off at Katerinska 15 for which he will die. It is
twenty to six may I use your toilet? Frau Brodt pales
hesitates upstairs she cries the last door on the

left on the left the last door on the left she cries it
he loudly climbs the stairs. Time. Schnittstelle
No. 5 *Untergeziefer* Friedrich flying down the stairs
die Toilette is doch voller Blut! The toilet bowl is full of
blood! Is somebody injured here? Are you hiding
somebody?

4

The Sun's Anemic Sheen On The Snow-Covered Slopes Of The Glarner Alps

The Speed of Falling

In the morning Frau Brodt
enters the room. In the evening Heinrich Krebernick
gets up from the kitchen stool. He feels the weight of
falling a tearing through whose threadbare slits he
feels the speed of all falling then it falls through his
body slightly slower than if he weren't holding it back
with the little matter that he is each thing is merely a
brief hindrance of a universal falling it would fall
unhindered in heaven he thinks while here all things
this chair or these blue irises in their tall tubular vase
on my small wooden table are merely variable
obstacles if the speed of falling in a stone were
approximately three hundred million (300000000)
times slower he speculates but what are numbers
than in an iris's petals where it enters and exits almost
unhindered which is why we love flowers. Takes off
his tie knitted

sweater vest shirt pants
and socks and folds them unnecessarily neatly over
the back of the chair in front of the window walks
across the room folds back. The sheet and comforter
of his narrow bed in his rented room three floors up in

the Diggelmans' stately chalet at Spitalstrasse 89 in
the town of Wetzikon and lies down in his underwear
it is the day of his death the 6th of December 1969. His
window looks

east he lifts his head and
briefly strains leaning on his right elbow to see the
evening sun's anemic sheen on the snow-covered
slopes of the majestic *Glarner Alpen* pointing with his
finger. He whispers *Mürtschenstock Fronalpstock
Rautispitz Vrenelisgärtli* [18] and when he says
Vrenelisgärtli he says *Miriam*. Still on his right elbow
he reaches into his bedside drawer grabs his
Dienstpistole which was returned to him after his
internment in Witzwil Prison and from which only one
shot had been fired on 12 February 1944 into
Untergeziefer Albert Friedrich's left breast pocket.
Switches it awkwardly from his left to his right hand
turns off the safety switch aims it and as if in
remembrance of Albert Friedrich's untimely death
fires into his own left chest. Then with his right hand
swings the gun in the radius of his stiffly outstretched
arm over his head and lands it with a thud on top of
the *Neue Revue* sporting a bare chested woman on his
bedside table pulls the sheet up to cover the spreading
stain of the wound on his white ribbed armless
undershirt and dies his eyes. Hard as pebbles

---

18 Names of some of the foremost peaks of the Glarner Alps

his hands symmetrically
curved over the edge of the sheet whose breaking in
the Columbia Concentration Camp in the Tempelhof
area had likely saved his life the hands that had held
Miriam's stump.

Miriam who meanwhile
lies ravaged in the knife and scissor sharpener's
writhing stone wheel by a decade of what was then
called shrinking of the brain her heart worn to the
bones. In room 113 in the *Sonnhalde Heim für
Betagte.* [19] And though she doesn't know that
Heinrich won't come home anymore she feels his
death sharp as a December draft in the sudden
solitude of her body each of whose parts to the
smallest epidermal plane and fold had by the touch of
his hands once been pronounced beautiful and dies
two months later in the same winter.

(Berlin 1933)

---

19 Nursing home in Grüningen near Zürich

Ribbons

And dies two months
later in the same winter. On the day before his death
he had bent his ear to her breath. His mouth to her ear
Miriam his left hand on the bed frame his right hand
curved like a garden hoe cupped over her stump
Miriam his ear on her mouth had she called him? He
leaves her head sidewise on the pillow her eyes follow
his receding shape through the open door down the
hall. He whispers to himself leans forward in his chair
takes off his socks throws his face up at the night
falling his hands hang on him a weight he has lifted
today he could not have lifted tomorrow.

He folds his clothes
unnecessarily neatly over the back of the chair and
briefly looks out east onto the sunlit slopes his gaze
soars over the high sharp horizon

up through the small
window of his cell approximately thirty-six years
earlier five wires slicing the sky into four horizontal
ribbons but what are numbers over the court of the
Columbia Concentration Camp he hears the cries the
shuffling the clanking the sobbing the knocking he

briefly cries pats his checkered sweater vest on the
chair straightens it once more smoothes out the
barking the breaking the slapping remembers the
door of his cell admitting four more politicals in the
course of the next weeks one of whom slurs and
whistles to this 6th day of December 1969 *nein nane*
through his crushed jaw *is Nerner Nussgaun* [20] and
chokes on his blood during his first night in the cell
where there is not enough floor space for three men to
lie down. Heinrich kneels his forehead on the cold
edge of the bed while his hands are examined by one
of the new arrivals one would have to break them
again he says to set them and winds

                         blue ribbons of sky torn
from Werner Nussbaum's shirt round each finger to
make them mend as straight as possible while
perhaps on the same day Miriam on her yellow bench
in *Tiergarten* weaves Heinrich's number through the
teeth of her comb or she stands in Feldkirch her name
changed to Herlinde Jung with the secret Ɔ at her
table rolling flour thin as lampshade.

                  When it had been only
months into his incarceration he had forgotten how
long the difference of the days marked only by the

---

20 My name is Werner Nussbaum.

changes of the color of the four ribbons of sky
between the five wires he is one early morning
dragged out of his cell an iron bucket wired to his
head sat on a chair to explain to *Obersturmgeziefer*
von Wiesenthal the disappearance of his fiancée
Miriam Stein while *Untergeziefer* (meanwhile)
Knebbel beats a hammer on the kettle Fräulein Stein
who has been convicted *in absentia* of collaboration
with the *Schweinehund* Pfenniger the *Hauswart* at
their once mutual domicile at Alte Jackobsstrasse of
hiding Jews and other criminal activities to be sure. *In
absentia?* Wafts Heinrich's voice from beneath the
bucket *dann weizz izz nizzt* the hammer *wo zie izt* zen
I zon't know where zhe iz his vowels dampened to an
echoing rumble between the hammer's ring his liquids
amplified to a hissing. And is made

                          to stand naked in the
court with the bucket on his head a day and a night
perhaps in September was it 1933? And hears the shots
at Spitalstrasse 89 on the third floor? Or is it in the
Columbia Concentration Camp? Aimed but he doesn't
know it under his bucket at *Schweinehund* Pfenniger's
left breast pocket? He is relieved. From standing in the
court only because of having as his records attest
attended night courses for an apprenticeship as an
electrician.

Hands

Because of having as his
records attest attended night courses for an
apprenticeship as an electrician he stands in the
distance between the chair with the folded clothes and
the sunlit slopes of the *Glarner Alpen* he lifts his hands
bandaged with ribbons of sky to the *Alpenglühn*.[21]
Welcher Idiot has done that pointing at his broken
hands? *Obergeziefer* Knebbel Heinrich says is
reprimanded for unwittingly restoring *Untergeziefer*
Knebbel's former rank slapped for snitching on a
member of the *Wehrmacht* and sentenced to death by
firing squad the next morning he can still repair. He
cries electrical

equipment and install
wiring *sehn sie doch Herr Obersturmgeziefer* my
thumb he shouts and forefinger and here my middle
finger I can bend them look I know how to is slapped
electrical! Answer when you are asked but thereafter
repairs lighting radios brittle wiring electric fencing

---

21 Literally, the glow of the evening sun on the alpine slopes

installs new wire lines and appliances for lighting
heating torturing cooking listening devices in

the knife and scissor
sharpener's stone wheel the permanent crook of his
little and ring fingers. Of his left hand turns out
advantageous to the *Reichs* business like a convenient
sleeve or catch for temporary retention say of a
screwdriver or a roll of wire a rubber band or a roll of
electrical tape while the forefinger middle finger and
thumb twist the copper threads of hot and cold wires.
Good work *Heilittla* Krebernick *Heilittla Herr
Untergeziefer* in October of 1936 his hands having

metamorphosed into
multiple slip joint pliers he is transferred though he
still wears a red triangle on his left breast pocket to
help prisoners of the Emsland camps in the
construction of the Sachsenhausen model
concentration camp thirty-five kilometers north of
Berlin (35 km) to learn what it means to refuse the
Nazi salute and immediately on pain of death to
report subversive *Ungereimtheiten*.[22]

---

22 Things that don't rhyme.

Night Sky

And immediately on
pain of death to report subversive *Ungereimtheiten*
though if he does he will have to report that he thinks
of Miriam waiting on her yellow bench in *Tiergarten*
his eyes open in the twilight of his Sachsenhausen cell
his head on the neatly folded jacket turned sideways
to the damp wall he is four years late perhaps five
while Miriam for all we know is rolling *Apfelstrudel*
thin as lampshade in Feldkirch. But one day let us say
13 November for convenience's sake but any date
would do he stands under his cell window stretches
his arms to the glass looks up at the fine-grained
northern sky and sees a fragment of a flock of geese
tootling southward in v-formation

and if his thoughts of
Miriam could have broken through the glass slipped
through the iron bars like angels born in his breath

and if his thoughts of
Miriam were thereupon borne skywards through the
five-wired sky to a height cold and distant as the light

of a spent star

and if Miriam had at that
same moment briefly stepped outside in Feldkirch
wiped her hands on her apron lighted a *Stella* and
jerked her match violently sideways

and if she had while
tossing the match into a bed of wilted geraniums
looked up at the night falling like shipwreck

her eyes would have held
in their gaze unbeknownst to her Heinrich's thought
of her in a wisp of ribboned night sky while beyond
the electric fence of Sachsenhausen Concentration
Camp the trees would have leaned sharply in the
incessant north wind.

North Wind

           The trees would have
leaned sharply in the incessant north wind the
triangle on his left breast pocket is ceremoniously
abgerissen. He has solemnly abjured his youthful
follies and with a small gaggle of ragged converts on
the main court of Sachenhausen it is summer of 1939
in a hasty ceremony among repeated shouts of
Heilittla click click *Heilittla* click Heinrich swears
allegiance to the *Führer* click is promoted because of
his expertise in matters electrical to *Untergeziefer*
Heilittla handed a *Walther P 38 Dienstpistole* and
shipped

           to Prague to oversee work
in the manufacturing of munitions in a camouflaged
warehouse appropriated from the Škoda Works in
Pilsen where on say the 12th of February 1944 let it be
a quarter past five a cold drizzle falling from the slate
sky *Untergeziefer* Krebernick climbs his bicycle and
rides back to his room at Katerinska 15 his hands
dreaming songbirds on the handlebars.

5

A Clownish Trio Of Saltimbanques Pirouetting On The Horizon

Blood

His hands dreaming
songbirds on the handlebars *Untergeziefer* Krebernick
leans his bicycle against the wall removes his leather
satchel from the rack and enters *Heilittla* there is
blood *Heilittla* one hundred five degrees (105°) in
the toilet she gives shelter to a partisan no doubt
perhaps even a *Judenschwein* we must *Untergeziefer*

Friedrich cannot finish his
sentence because he is dead in the updraft of the
wings' stroke they stand mute darkwards listening if anyone might have
heard the shot but no sound of knocking no inquiries no
truckload of SS *Geziefer* all lies as still as Albert
Friedrich's prostrate uniform with him inside of it
their only hiding place is a few hours of night Heinrich
calls softly

up the stairs Miriam slap-
top-slap-top-slap coming down the stairs with her
cane click *um Himmelswillen! Was ist passiert?* Since the
search party will first be dispatched to the
camouflaged warehouse where *Untergeziefer*

Friedrich is supposed to have dropped off the files then surely to *Untergeziefer* Krebernick's address at Katerinska 15 where he rents a room from a certain Frau Brodt the files have spilled onto the floor.

Wheel

The files have spilled onto
the floor five names of politicals in the camouflaged
warehouse lie open to the vast night into which they
are to be sent and the same night is falling fast in the
stone wheel and the wheel sings its refrain to keep the
sum of suffering a constant the logic of which is:

Had Frau Brodt reported
Untergeziefer Krebernick's violation of the Racial
Purity Law she would not have contracted his
pneumonia and died in a cellar in Hluboš because he
would have died of it in the Ardennes but since he will
not die in the Ardennes his pneumonia is lying
unclaimed as if on a shelf waiting for a host. Miriam

while he burns the files in
the kitchen stove Miriam hide and hunger in cellars
and haylofts in Hluboš Čimelice Kraselov Kubova Huť
in Ulrichsberg. They flee south towards Austria
hidden by farmers hungered by soldiers fed by
kindness terrified by the knife and scissor sharpener's
stone wheel whistling the refrain of the suffering

of Frau Brodt in a cellar in Hluboš of Herman and Elfriede Knell hanged in the *Spazierhof* of the *Justizanstalt* in Feldkirch of the monkeys who were slain for having been taught the Hitler salute of Werner Nussbaum who choked on his blood in a cell of the Columbia Concentration Camp in the Tempelhof area of *Untergeziefer* Knebbel who lost his eyes and hands for Hitler and who forgot Miriam's phone number in his pocket to save her life of the Jesuit priest who forged Miriam's passport of the 110 of whom Herlinde Jung was one injured in the bombing of *Reservelazaret 1 Antoniushaus* in Feldkirch of *Untergeziefer* Albert Friedrich though he suffered only his death of *Schweinehund* Pfenniger who was shot for hiding Jews while Heinrich for all we know stood in the same court naked with a bucket wired to his head of a young Nazi's mother and sister whose names we do not know and who will yet have to die in the bombing of Salzburg of Sarah Rebecka and Ruth who were found dead in the ruins of the Fröhlichs' *Metzgerei* of Marlene a partisan from Bregenz who does not know that she will be tortured by the Gestapo and let us not forget Karl Schreber who worked in the *Spinnerei* in Feldkirch and must have thought he was to receive an *Auszeichnung* or the sixteen-

year-old member of the
Czech partisans in Vimperk who will hanging by his
arms ripped out of their shoulder sockets betray
Heinrich and Miriam's hiding place.

Scherenschnitt [23]

Or the sixteen-year-old
member of the Czech partisans in Vimperk who will
hanging by his arms ripped out of their shoulder
sockets betray Heinrich and Miriam's hiding place in a
Scherenschnitt

the three. Would have cut
a clownish trio of *saltimbanques* [24] pirouetting on the
horizon Heinrich fiercely pedaling in Frau Brodt's late
husband's incongruous pants and coat Miriam
astride the rear rack of Heinrich's bicycle playing her
rented zither Frau Brodt on her bicycle coughing

rose petals in a few hours
there is no telling how many search parties will comb
the city to account for Miriam's second day missing at
U Nemocnice 2, 128 Hospital Heinrich's mysterious
absence at the camouflaged warehouse *Untergeziefer*
Friedrich's failure to return to the barracks the night
before while Frau Brodt whose disappearance will

---

23 Scissor-cut
24 Traveling circus artists

only be noted once the SS arrive at Katerinska 15 drags stops puts her head on her handlebars hangs in her bicycle pale and feverish. In Rudná barely outside of Prague they discard their bicycles behind a barn climb hastily into the back of a parked truck pointing south its two-stroke engine idling *cluckcluck cluckcluck cluckcluck* soon they hear the truck door open and slam shut the truck lurches into gear. Early

morning shudders to a halt the drizzle has ceased coughing who is there? Is there someone? The driver has come around lifts the tarp aha *Kdo je tady?* Who is this? Draws on his cigar shrugs his shoulders points his finger in the direction of the church tower on a hill outside the small village and walks in a cloud of smoke to a nearby house. Heinrich sounds the massive brass knocker on the double doors of the priest's house *Juden?* Behind one of the doors slightly ajar Jesuskillers go get yourself

hanged slams. The door I am not Frau Brodt doesn't finish her sentence covers her mouth bends over coughs a volley of blood into her coat sleeve hangs on Heinrich's arm they stumble through the glistening streets in the fine-grained light of early morning.

Light

On Heinrich's arm they
stumble through the glistening streets in the fine-
grained light of early morning hear the clanking of a
milk pail in an open door *Mein Gott* can I help you?
Gottseidank! Sprechen sie Deutsch? Mein Gott you are
completely wet. I can let you get dry in my house
where are we? You don't know? In Hluboš come in
but you are terribly *ach du meine Güte!* Miriam
bending over Frau Brodt coughing gurgling wheezing
moaning thrashes that afternoon in a high fever
Miriam wipes her face with a washcloth Heinrich
pacing peers through the windows. Frau Slezák
comes running into the room wringing her hands you
must leave at once you must leave they are looking for
three dangerous fugitives she pales shaking wanted
hesitates

for murder of a *Wehr-*
machtsgeziefer in Prague they are knocking on all
doors. And since we do not have an answer to the
question why they should be lucky why not have them
be arrested to assure the orderliness of the process

Fräulein Stein to be heaved footless into a cattle car on a long train of cattle cars to die less than an hour into the ride or to die in a small room overlooking the pretty village square in Theresienstadt at sunset say or shortly after arriving on the long Birkenau platform where she hardly has to walk or be carried more than a few hundred steps to the gas chambers under the slack sky *Untergeziefer* Krebernick to be summarily executed though his one death could hardly compensate for no fewer than four charges namely 1. desertion 2. high treason 3. murder and 4. *Rassenschande* Frau Bedřiška Brodt sent to prison in Prague to be hanged but

                      wait *um Himmels Willen*
Frau Slezák we can't leave in broad daylight they descend the steep wooden stairs into the cellar and huddle behind a shelf filled with empty canning jars. That evening they have wrapped and packed their few things rented zither among them and are climbing the stairs like frogs in a weather glass a sharp rattle of knocks *Aufmachen!!* Back downstairs down! Go down! Frau Brodt coughs hunched on the cellar steps you must stop

                      her cough Herr
Krebernick Miriam slides down the stairs on her hands and legs to the clattering of her cane Heinrich

carries Frau Brodt back behind the canning shelf they hear Frau Slezák open the door *Heilittla you speak German?* Heavy booted steps on the wooden floor above the cellar *der Keller machen sie mal auf!* The cellar open it! *Licht!*

Earth

Licht! The white winged
ceramic switch held in the ceramic socket by a brass
screw is turned nothing is turned nothing. The bulb
lies warm in Heinrich's hand don't even breathe a
heavy. Coat pressed over Frau Brodt's face
Taschenlampe! Does anyone have a pocket light? And
if the beam had pierced the darkness the three
fugitives would have floated in a kaleidoscope of
canning jars but no flashlight could be found *im
Tausendjährigen Reich. Ruhe!* Silence! They stand as if
choreographed by an intendant of a small chamber
play

listening at the top of the
stairs a dog barks outside stand keep standing steps
Heilittla the door. The coat removed Frau Brodt's eyes
a vast horizon. That night Heinrich digs the earth deep
in Frau Slezák's backyard slides the length of Frau
Brodt's body into the ditch and discards in a flurry of
moonlight the surplus soil the volume of which if one
were to have it weighed and measured would exactly
equal Frau Brodt's weight and bodily density all taken

into account and by which correspondence the secrecy of her absconding to all appearance lies open to this day under the sky in the tiny village of Hluboš evenly scattered among the wilted stalks of cauliflower and cabbage.

6

The Water Nymphs Come Out And Bathe In The Moonlight

Snow

Evenly scattered among
the wilted stalks of cauliflower and cabbage they step
into the night. Leaving Hluboš south they come upon
a *Puch* motorcycle the key in the ignition hole on top
of the headlamp beside a darkened house. Miriam
climbs into the sidecar Heinrich pushes her quietly
past the sleeping houses kick starts the engine well
south of Hluboš blubbers dies tries again tries again
opens the tank top shakes the motorcycle from side to
side shoves it off the road walks back to Hluboš
punctures the gas line of a parked truck with his
pocket knife and returns with a milk bucket of
gasoline the lights. Of a car approaching

from behind a bend in the
road Heinrich leaps into a ditch spills the gasoline the
car slows stops *was machen sie denn da?* What are you
up to there? Come out stand up man! The officer in
Wehrmachtsuniform has stepped out of the car the
engine idling Heinrich's *Dienstpistole* unprofitably in
his satchel in the *Puchs* sidecar step in front of my
headlights so I can see you *Name? Papiere?* And who

are you? Miriam has limped towards them *bitte lassen sie uns gehen* please let us go she pleads they stand still as two birds painted in flight are you injured? No she blushes lowers her head I lost my *nu* I lost

my foot in a bombing. The officer studies them *Juden?* No he is not yes I am no you are not yes we are both *Judenschweine* Heinrich shouts silence! Step into the car here you up here with me you Fräulein Stein in the back seat *ach* why don't you both sit in the back and don't worry about your *Dienstpistole Untergeziefer* Krebernick you don't need it tonight. How do you know

our names? Takes no genius to figure that out lucky you to run into me I will keep the secret of your escape with some secrets of my own and drop you off with some people who will take you to a safe place. I can only drive you to Čimelice. From there you need to take the train I know someone who can get you to travel secretly but only to Vimperk if you are warmly enough dressed. From there you will need to get yourself to a small village Klaffer am Hochficht hard to get to across the border but the only place where you can be picked up by partisans. He puts the car into gear *vielen Dank* Miriam sobs collapsed against the back of the front seat how can we

88

thank you says Heinrich
having retrieved his satchel a car approaches from the
opposite side hide under that blanket you lie on the
floor here the car slows the windows are lowered
alles ok? Alles ok! Both cars accelerate in opposite
directions. They travel in silence Miriam asleep on the
back seat dreams the weight of falling

the room into which she
walks falling the table the chairs falling the tubular
vase six irises blue as night falling and the weight of
death in the room and the dark presses in against the
windows like wind made of darkness and how she
asks in her dream when I cannot walk with my lost
foot and arrive in Čimelice well after midnight. Before
Heinrich and Miriam are dropped off near the station
under the awnings of a storage shed the officer pulls
Miriam aside here is an address in Klaffer am
Hochficht the *ch's* and *f's* hissing from his mouth
memorize it don't share it with Krebernick in case you
get caught it is less likely they will assume you know
anything or torture you rather than him though I'm
sorry to say this is far from certain. Leads her back to
Heinrich wait until morning someone will come to
take you to a cattle car the code word is your address
in Prague the man probably won't speak German and
what is your name *bitte?* Asks Miriam no names the

less you know the better and keep your

secret Fräulein. Here take
this. Blanket and some money here you will need it
they sit shivering the blanket wrapped around
themselves on a cart holding each other why did he
tell you to keep a secret what did he say to you? Only
to remind you *nu* to be careful with your *Dienspistole*
though she could tell him that goodness is not
goodness if it is not a secret her eyes dark as falling he
pulls her head towards him the snow falls in thick wet
flakes.

Die Moldau [25]

                The snow falls in thick
wet flakes they wait it is late morning people glancing
at them no one is coming *mein Gott* Heinrich we are
betrayed Heinrich walks to the station building back
to Miriam don't keep going to the building Heinrich
you will be arrested he walks back. It is past noon
Miriam has stepped

                        under a chestnut tree
slips and falls is helped up by a woman. With a
headscarf who whispers *Katrinska patnáct* [26] where is
Heinrich? They wait he is they can see it questioned
by a policeman who wants papers. Heinrich points his
hand away from the shed where Miriam and the
woman are waiting while the moon hangs in a pale
white wisp of a sickle in the sky walks with the
policeman in the direction towards stacks of firewood
they disappear and after

---

25 The most famous of the six symphonic poems of *Má Vlast*
(Homeland) composed between 1874 and 1879 by the Czech
composer Bedřich Smetana
26 Katerinska 15

approximately five
minutes but what are numbers Heinrich reappears
without the policeman limps leisurely towards the
shed lights as if to mock the gods of fortune a cigarette
on the platform and strolls back to Miriam we
must run he whispers panicked run who are you?
Katrinska patnáct the woman responds takes Miriam's
hand and drags her hurriedly away Heinrich bleeding
on his hands his hair matted with blood Miriam
stumbles is lifted onto her feet my cane don't let me lose
my cane they cross the tracks up from the station run
if that is the word back down in the direction towards
the station but on the far side of the parallel tracks
hidden by parked railroad cars cross the rails again
slide under one standing train Miriam towed and
heaved her stump bleeding in the socket reach a cattle
car her cane whose door.

Opens to a knock in the
rhythm of the stately bars of Smetana's *Die Moldau*

Miriam and Heinrich are hauled in by outstretched
arms and hands the woman has vanished before they
could thank her and sit among a group of tattered
refugees Jews gypsies women men two or three

children silently huddled on the rough wooden planks
an hour passes perhaps two what does it matter the
train sways into motion Miriam hears the light
rippling waters of the mountain springs.

The train moves at a snail's
pace stops stands belching and hissing for hours in the
cold damp air Miriam head tilted eyes closed lies in
Heinrich's arms hears the jubilant hunters the polka
rhythm of the village wedding before it jerks on when
it reaches speed the draft makes them huddle in knots
over each other the water nymphs come out and bathe
in the moonlight despite the stench and grime from
urine and excrement that clings to clothes and
blankets and hears the sumptuous cadences of the
Vltava flowing through Prague past the castle of
Vyšehrad.

Milk Light

          And hears the sumptuous
cadences of the Vltava flowing through Prague past
the castle of Vyšehrad. Night falls early the train
comes to a screeching stop in a thickly wooded area
the engine drumming and coughing not a sound don't
make a sound everything has to be done quietly and
quick a knock in the rhythm of the stately bars of *Die
Moldau* one of the refugees slowly opens the door
they all slip outside aided by a small group of
partisans swallowed by the dark of the forest stumble
through the trees some carrying children old people
leaning on and dragged along by younger ones they
arrive at a farmhouse all in the dark a few are allowed
to stay while others climb onto horse-drawn carts to
destinations of which the common denominator is
only that it is unknown and for the time

                    being perhaps safe
enough. Heinrich and Miriam are taken to the town of
Vimperk on a motorcycle Miriam sitting astride on the
gas tank in front leaning on her zither case shivering
uncontrollably Heinrich on the back seat the young

man who drives the motorcycle speaks German tells
them his head sideways so Heinrich can hear him in
the rush of the wind that they can stay in Vimperk
only briefly and need to find transportation to
Haidmühle where they will be able to hide
several nights if all goes well hardly. Arrived and
settled for the night in a drafty shed they are
awakened

in the dark *schnell schnell*
you must leave our action was discovered the Nazis
are searching addresses. They steal along alleys and
streets Heinrich carrying Miriam on his back in the
milk of the new day leave Vimperk behind them and
spend the day in a hayloft south of town above a
stable the warmth of the cows wafting up through the
cracks in the floor Miriam quietly moaning their
young partisan how old are you? Sixteen I can't tell
you my name I will try to find help in town they will
come in the night.

Miriam Dreams and Does Not Remember Her
Dream the Next Morning

They come in the night in
my hands the stones for proof from the fallen houses
and the burnt cellars from my hands the cries

of children into the
ribbons of the sky into the night sky our cries into the
sounds of the names of towns and rivers my cries
from the opened hands I pour them out I hold my
hands out

I have put my children to
bed in the shoveled pits hear my lullabies look a
feathering see the wisp my foot my falling look they
come tear the flesh and bone from my body and the
stars from my hands for proof of burning.

Silent Night

For proof of burning
Heinrich and Miriam wait the day and through the
night and the next day they haven't eaten. In the dusk
they slip out of the barn Miriam's stump bleeding
from the chafing drags behind Heinrich trying to keep
away from the farmhouse where the dogs barking and
growling leap at them Miriam drops her cane holds
her zither case to protect herself light falls out

of a door in a long square
sheath a man stands in it whistles his dogs back eyes
them suspiciously beckons them to approach are you
injured Fräulein no I have she blushes lowers her
head *nu* a wooden his wife appears leg wiping her
hands on her apron *Um Gottes Willen so können Sie
doch nicht unterwegs sein* my God you can't travel like
that come in *sind sie Juden?* No answer. No one came
to pick you up in the hayloft? *Mein Gott!* The farmer
looks worriedly up and down the empty street *bitte*
they eat

Brotknödel in a dark

brown meat sauce with red cabbage sleep on the attic
floor we don't have much space please be quiet my
wife's mother is upstairs bedridden she might
sympathize with the Nazis we don't know she just
moved in with us after the death of her husband what
is that knocking on the floor Pavel? Nothing mother
I'm moving a chair she can't know you are hiding here
they slide silently past the closed bedroom door
Miriam carried in the regal movements of *Die Moldau*
before she falls asleep and the night turns on its
hinges

                    leans it does not fall its
lights cold and distant with gloamings and helmets of
radius bright to the eye needled in the dark and
washed of all purpose those who lie in their sleep those
who find themselves in grieved thought those in
whom time falls like something falling slightly
detained briefly arrested by what was it? A little
matter the envy of the dark car lights reaching
through it sounds coming across

                    by voices below
aufmachen! Open the door is loudly breached a black
booted SS with a contingent of *Wehrmachtsgeziefer*
steps in are you Pavel Čermák we must search nothing
in the hayloft Herr *Untersturmgeziefer* your house!
Search the cellar! Nothing. The attic! They climb the

stairs stand in the dark shine their flashlights into
cobwebs and corners move furniture crates boxes
Herr *Untersturmgeziefer* a zither the case not even
dusty! Who plays the zither here? My mother calls
Frau Čermák from below I just put it up in the attic
this afternoon she is sick in bed with a high fever.
Good let us hear her play that will help her get better
they carry the zither

                              down from the attic enter
the room play us something! The old woman
disheveled feverish sits up in her bed rubs her eyes
her hands hovering over the zither case opens it takes
the zither out puts the plectrum on her thumb and
haltingly plays *Pásli ovce valaši.* [27] Struck mute they
stand in silence and let her play to the end Frau
Čermák frozen to the floor her hand on her mouth.
Půjdem spolu do Betléma next? The old woman coughs
into the sleeve of her nightgown or perhaps *Tichá
noc?* [28] *Heilittla* click forgive the disturbance. Search

                         the hayloft once more!
Smartly bow click and leave. Pavel Čermák runs back
up to the attic where Heinrich is helping Miriam climb

---

27 "The men from Valassko are taking sheep out," traditional
Bohemian Christmas carol
28 "Let's all go to Bethlehem," "Silent Night," traditional Bohemi-
an Christmas carols

back in through the small roof window from a world
briefly outside of history.

Fastnacht [29]

From a world briefly
outside of history. How they crossed the border after
their stay with the Čermák family south of Vimperk by
what means they traveled during those days and
nights of cold and rain and snow how they managed to
beg or steal food along the way the nameless
Geziefer's money having long been spent neither
could remember. It is perhaps in Haidemühle where
they were briefly sighted a wretched pair of
reprobates to be sure by the mere looks of them and
duly reported to the authorities weary of swindling
Jews or Gypsies what is most likely. Is only that they
must

have been reported
somewhere along the Austrian border separated and
detained Miriam rounded up with a group of Jews
who had somehow one does not want to know how
managed to survive years of persecution all to be
death marched north to Theresienstadt. Heinrich who
has

---

29 Traditional carnival during Lent

no papers and gives his
name as Rudolf von Reichsthal hoping to get some
mileage out of the aristocratic name is held in a
municipal prison beaten with an electric cable and
rightly suspected to be a deserter one is going to get
to the bottom of this with *deutscher Gründlichkeit.*
Miriam meanwhile found to be incapable of surviving
the forced march to Theresienstadt is slated for
execution in a nearby clearing in the woods or they
are not

reported or if reported
not apprehended or if apprehended inexplicably
released by some bureaucratic mishap or perhaps
they are found never to have loafed and dallied in
Haidmühle as they would have been charged what do
we know but having arrived in Nová Pec cane and
rented zither included where the *Fastnacht* revelers to
all appearance have managed to set a barn on fire and
provided the necessary distraction to have a
Wehrmachts BMW with sidecar stolen which the
thieves ride noisily through the unguarded border to
Ulrichsberg.

7

The Air A Cold Slap The Sky Slate And A Light Rain

Partisans

Noisily through the
unguarded border to Ulrichsberg Miriam beware the
colorfully uniformed medalled veterans of the
Wehrmacht and the *Waffen SS* [30] are drinking and
giving speeches awake let us take your zither flee
towards Aigen along the Grosse Mühl Fluss with its
leaves shingled at the bottom by the current watch for
contingents of *Wehrmachtsgeziefer* in the rain
wrapped in fear and hunger and each other's arms in
cellars attics haylofts under bridges in abandoned
houses barns cross the weight of rivers the weight of
fields in starweight the sudden bends in the street the
weight of fear the weight of hunger to Klaffer

am Hochficht and the
weight of the body in the socket climb through
cathedrals of redwood the night having ceased and the
high light of quiet above and their coming onto a field
and their eyes still and the secret address stay three

---

30 The Ulrichsberg gathering is an annual reunion since 1958 for
veterans of the *Wehrmacht* and *Waffen SS*.

nights hide in a small but heated back room owned by
a blacksmith who repairs Miriam's rusting hinges a
knock in the

night no names. Nor
do we know how they were taken to a house near Linz
they arrive eyes bandaged as they near their destination
and spend the year until November undiscovered in
an attic. During the summer the temperature rises to
tropical degrees but in the late evenings they are
sometimes allowed to visit downstairs where they
can walk

upright sometimes to eat
a warm meal still no names good works. Are nameless
because if they happen in such evil times *es verschlägt
einem geradezu die Sprache* one is altogether
speechless. Miriam her eyes dark as falling plays her
rented zither she is pregnant in the third

month without touching
its strings her hands are birds perfectly hovering five
centimeters (5 cm) over the instrument her fingers
rhythmically plucking the air so the twigs won't break
out of her elbows they cannot stay. Papers are forged
Heinrich with moustache Miriam's black hair dyed
blonde *nu* I sleep with Hitler he should be put to death
for *Rassenschande* she smiles at his moustache on the

17th of November. They are put on the train to Salzburg. From there to Innsbruck from there to Bregenz where they hope to make their escape with the help of the *Partisanen* across the *Bodensee* to Switzerland. In Salzburg. The conductor looks at Miriam's passport.

Bombs

The conductor looks at
Miriam's passport. Shakes his head slaps the passport
with his left hand into the palm slap slap slap of his
right hand and orders them to come to the sirens
1216 bombs scream from the sky leave the train
crawl underneath wait stay don't get the zither
Heinrich gets the suitcase the cane and the zither glass
flying they spend the night in the crowded *Wartesaal*
where the windows have been blown out the
conductor if he has survived still has Miriam's
passport if the passport is in one piece then another
night then perhaps another who wants to keep track
they have eaten pork sausages with bread and
sauerkraut they are now almost out of the money
given to them Miriam pale as November shaking
Heinrich goes to the *Fundbüro geschlossen. Melden
sie sich bei der Schutzstaffel gegenüber dem Bahnhof!*
Lost and Found closed. For lost items report to the SS
office facing the station terrified walks to the office
where he miraculously retrieves the passport my wife is

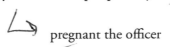 pregnant the officer

Nazi! (handwritten annotation above "Wehrmachtsgeziefer")

a young *Wehrmachtsgeziefer* with swollen red eyes
perhaps because he just got word of his mother's and
sister's deaths in the bombing which is to show that
death can lead to miraculous retrievals of passports
and that good and evil are bedfellows even as we here
don't quite know to whom to assign which attribution
they get on a crowded train to Innsbruck bombs. Will
be falling here too exactly twelve minutes after the
train pulls out of the station towards Bregenz Miriam
sitting on the suitcase shaking. In Bregenz

                  they have an address
Schlossergasse 17 no one answers their knocking a
neighbor opens a window and whispers *verschwunden
die sind einfach verschwunden.*[31] They go around the
house through a garden gate Heinrich pries open a
window climbs through lets Miriam in

                  the house is ransacked
broken glass paper dishes clothes whole cupboards
toppled over beds turned upside down *mein Gott* we
can't stay here but where shall we go look there are
potatoes here a speck of butter a head of cauliflower
somebody at the back door very quietly *bitte kein Lärm* please no
noise waves beckons with his hand finger on his lips
come you can't stay here no leave the food just as you
found it they leave Miriam

---

31 Disappeared, they simply disappeared.

shaking near fainting
follow me across the back yard climb over a low fence
and now just walk normally I'll walk ahead of you
Heinrich carrying Miriam on his back and leads them
to a house through a gate on the side of the house to
the backyard a woman opens the back door casts her
eyes about pulls Miriam in by her shoulder she falls
the man. Has disappeared Heinrich lifts

her to her feet and holds
her. They were betrayed I am Marlene the only one
left in Bregenz the others were able to escape across
the lake who knows where here you need to lie down
food yes I have potatoes and cabbage even a bit of
bacon. They wake Miriam up to eat.

Stecken [32]

        They wake Miriam up to eat. In the morning they find the man who owns the boat he wants 500 *Schilling* for each I am not Pestalozzi [33] I have a family too and if I get caught he throws up his arms I take *Franken* too 100 each if you don't have *Schilling* Miriam begs him *um Himmels Willen* for heaven's sake do not let us be arrested and killed he eyes her up and down a *Holzbein?* [34] How did you get that? Laughs where is it cut you still have your thigh? Lights a cigar I will take him too if you

        touches her thigh with the back of his hand makes a gesture with his finger these are he says bad times Heinrich pulls Miriam out they fight in a nearby alley he will take us once he knows I'm pregnant she whispers her forehead against his chest he will let us go with him I will not let him you will not I am not a pimp I am not a whore but I can help us live Heinrich Heinrich she

---

32 Stick
33 Benevolent Swiss pedagogue and educational reformer (1746 –1827)
34 Wooden leg

pleads fiercely goes back
to the boathouse I'm pregnant in the third month *bitte*
would you really want to do this with a Jew she pales
as she hears herself say it you are just saying this to
get away *gratis* no I cannot please no I'll scream he
holds her

                       throat she thrashes drops
her cane hangs he gropes her up and down you are
thin as a *Stecken* there is no woman on your bones but
you can still put this for 500 *Schilling* you slut in your
mouth no please I can't he slaps her face talk dirty to
me you whore *ja* I will talk dirty I have taken teeth
jaws eyes ears fingers flaps of skin penises hands feet
bones to the *Antoniushaus Krematorium* in Feldkirch I
have taken teeth jaws eyes ears fingers flaps of skin
penises hands feet bones to the *Krematorium* of U
Nemocnice 2, 128 Hospital in Prague if you want me
to talk dirty I have heard a man speak without lips I
have heard a man scream Hitler gib mir meine Augen zurück
she whispers it he slaps. Her

                       hard throws her down
rips her skirt off dumps the reeking weight of himself
on her rides and plunders hides crouching in the alley
behind the boathouse rises leans against the stone
wall clings to it her hands bleeding from the stone
clutches her torn skirt her cane limps back to Heinrich

who paces runs to her and holds her I would rather
die with you than live like this.

The Boat

                           I would rather die with
you than live like this. No we need his boat we can
just take it no we need to hide in it Heinrich she sobs I
can get us to Switzerland in his boat no the Germans
will find us Heinrich paces drawing fiercely on the
cigarette in his fingers bent like the blades of a garden
hoe we must return to the house to retrieve the
suitcase and your zither they see a car parked outside
Marlene. Taken by two men my zither no we can't
risk going in we must hurry Heinrich he will leave
with his boat without us to the boathouse with
nothing but their lives except Heinrich's *P 38* from
which only one shot has been fired at a quarter to six
on 12 February 1944 into *Untergeziefer* Albert
Friedrich's left breast pocket. Ah die *Judenhure* the
Jewish whore Heinrich aims. The gun turns the safety

                           switch off you *Scheisskerl*
you sorry shit hide us in your boat take us to
Switzerland or die with us right here one hour into the
ride the air a cold slap the sky slate and a light rain
Heinrich shoots him drops his body into the water or

he shoots him once they arrive early the next morning
or they remain cramped under deck

                    until they are dumped in a
field slightly east of Rorschach too close to the town
we are too close to those houses Heinrich aims his gun
so they hear the shot if you try to shoot me
Judenschwein Heinrich *mein Gott* don't shoot him
they'll hear the shot Miriam

                    drags her foot hangs on
her cane shaking. They are arrested less than an hour
after their arrival. *Untergeziefer* Krebernick to all
appearances a deserter is declared a prisoner of war
shipped to a prison in Witzwil he holds. Miriam holds
her and will not let go two. Policemen loosen their
arms as he is led away he points his pronged finger
across the small port of Rorschach. To a fishing boat

                    that's the smuggler who
took 500 *Schilling* from each of us if you care. Miriam
sits in front of an officer of the *Fremdenpolizei* [35]
awaiting deportation back to Germany because the
quota of refugees *es tut mir leid* I am sorry Frau
Krebernick he moves his *Villiger* to the corner of his
mouth has been limited by law. He gets up his *Villiger*

---

35 Police unit charged to enforce Swiss immigration laws

has died. *Das Boot* he says takes a matchbox from his
desk drawer studies the dead end of his cigar lights a
match *ist voll* [36] the blood on Miriam's chair.

---

36 The boat is full. Bundesrat von Steiger's metaphor for Switzer-
land's rigorous enforcement of its asylum policies during WWII

Blood

The blood on Miriam's chair runs on the floor a stretcher is brought in she is taken to the hospital in Romanshorn stays two weeks bleeds until she is mottled marble thanks to. Dr. Bietenholz's appeal granted asylum given a new prosthetic foot how could you have endured such a long journey with a leg like that? It is a miracle the 500 *Schilling* are returned to her having been obtained not apparently without difficulties from the smuggler Herr Krebernick will get his money back too she is told now I'm really

a whore she thinks but there are no miracles other than those because no hands hold her hunched over a box of cauliflower at *Maggi Suppen* in Kemptthal. Her hair is black she smokes her *Stellas* and relieves her twitching with disproportional jerkings of her arms when she extinguishes the match. She has bought herself a used zither from a music shop in Marktgasse 47 Winterthur where she rents a room with no tree in front.

Elijah

A music shop in Marktgasse 47 Winterthur where she rents a room with no tree in front. After the war Heinrich is released. And deported to Germany from where he repeatedly applies for a visa to visit his fiancée in Winterthur which finally granted allows him to buy a train ticket he has saved his 500 *Schilling* exchanged into Swiss currency she leaves *Maggi Suppen* at noon on Saturday. He stands with his umbrella. In the steady rain she sees him runs if we can call it that on the wet pavement he drops his umbrella lifts her into the air and if there had been an equivalent for their joy one would have said they were both taken up into the heavens by the force of his lifting like Elijah in the Bible. Miriam bends her leg

at the knee. So that Heinrich can hold her stump through the night in her room at Marktgasse 47 which holding is the closest equivalent we have in the material realm of Elijah's miracle for they were to the angels' envy one might

say that night taken up into the heavens and never
seen again.

(Aathal 1946)

By the end of the month
they move to Aathal a small damp town in a narrow
dark valley in the Zürich highlands where he obtains
work in the *Spinnerei Streiff* which is a miracle only a
little smaller given the cramped propriety of the Swiss

in bureaucratic matters and I am born Stern
Krebernick. Whose voice you read.

BIRDS LIKE SMALL DISHES RATTLING IN A CUPBOARD

Birthday

I am born Stern
Krebernick. Whose voice you read *Untergeziefer*
Knebbel shouts in the kitchen **Hitler gib mir meine
Augen zurück** vomits bent and shaking over the
kitchen sink hides my mother under the table on my
6th birthday. *Dann war noch der* she draws hard on
her *Stella dem die Lippen abgeschossen warn* then
there was the one whose lips had been shot off and he
had to talk through his teeth grabs my shoulder *nu* try
to say sonthing nithout your liggs and you see how
hard it is perhaps she would stop shaking if I could
and crawls out from under the table the airplanes a
distant whine. Let us say shortly later the same year?
Say two months or is it earlier or on the same day but
what are

days and years? She gives
me away on the telephone by the cellar steps because
the wiring runs through the cellar she has lifted the
heavy black receiver off its silvery hook and talks with
the orphanage Stern has been bad and spilt candle wax
from the birthday cake on the carpet I sit on the
wooden. Stairs to my room upstairs around the

corner of the hall and hear the yellow little car *s'gäle
Wäggeli* will come to get you tonight

                                maybe tomorrow but
what are days? She gives her body a shove to sync the
tremors sits down puts the plectrum on her thumb
starts playing *ombra mai fu* stops starts over
smoothes her skirt with both hands *Stella* erect
between her fore and middle fingers the burning end
traveling in a horizontal line down her skirt up and
down as if drawn by a yellow pencil if she puts it
down she will not find it again lights another one the
stubs. Glow like astral constellations in the house
plays *ombra mai fu* her head floats on her body a
pillow of sleepless nights stops gets up paces from the
zither to the cellar steps from the cellar steps to the
zither I follow her like twine loosened from a spool.
Untergeziefer Knebbel meanwhile

                                who once forgot Miriam's
phone number in his pocket to save her life must have
moved to Klagenfurt in Austria because on 24 August
1994 I arrive in Graz and read in the newspaper that
he is blinded again and that both of his hands are

newly *abgerissen* [37] I lie *im Gasthaus zur Steierstub'n*
Lendplatz 8 room 3 shaking

                       Miriam's *Kriegszittern*
through the night I stand by the window look up at the
falling of all things born like paper I cannot smooth
this paper here with my hands.

---

37 Torn off. A few days earlier the Klagenfurter policeman Theo
Kelz had lost both his hands and his eyesight through a pipe bomb.
Later, his sight was restored to him and he received two new hand
transplants.
See http://www.kleinezeitung.at/k/kaernten/feldkirchen/4107869

Apfelstrudel

I cannot smooth this
paper here with my hands and jerk my hands from left
to right. She pours her flour onto a small wooden
table to make *Apfelstrudel* rolls her dough it does not
tear when she pours in the apple slices raisins nuts
sugar and cinnamon rolls it all up in a hose of
unleavened dough thin as lampshade the length of our
table she sways. From foot to wooden foot I stand my
head over

the level of the table to
learn how to make a thing out of flour and pain. If
history she says were not made by men who are swine
because they don't wash their hands she lights a *Stella*
jerks her hand sideways after they piss but by women *nu*
we would if nothing else no longer need the smirking
politicians who shake their dirty hands after the *Krieg* [38]
and waggle

---

38 War

their heads on the
newsreels while their children are having their faces
eaten and their hands *abgerissen* and what of this?

Bird

Their children are having
their faces eaten and their hands *abgerissen* and what
of this? She says. To herself stops I cannot knead it
without drowning a bird with feathers the color of my
hair spotted with plaster dust looks

at her fluttering hands it
drowns and a small wound opens on the wing side she
turns her left hand its beak is bent to the blood hole
she lifts her hand to her face the bird draws out the
sounds of falling houses she hears the water. Into
which she falls the bombs

fall in her hands the stars
for proof of drowning from the fallen houses and the
burnt cellars. From her hands the cries of children
into the gray ribbons of the northern sky. Into the
night sky my father's cries. Into the sounds of the
names of Polish towns their cries from her opened
hands. Swings with Heinrich in the Spree with the
shingled leaves at the bottom stands on her foot sighs
squeezes her *Stella* into the ashtray plunges her hands

back into the dough and kneads it is worse. It is a dough into which is kneaded all the earth that holds the bodies.

Duden

        It is a dough into which is
kneaded all the earth that holds the bodies I lie on my
stomach on top of the apple rack in the cellar because
of the bust bodice the stocking suspender (Plate 13)
and the groin (Plate 2) *la région inguinale die
Leistengegend*. I turn the pages of the *Duden*[39] to Plate
6 H no. 12: the names of the artificial leg in four
languages:

1. *la jambe artificielle (la protèse de la jambe)*
2. *das Kunstbein (das künstliche Bein, die Beinprothese)*
3. *la gamba artificiale (la protesi)*
4. *la pierna artificial (la pierna protética u ortopédica)*

I copy into my notebook after (Plate 205) where I
sketched *der gespickte Hase* the larded hare on the
rack ladder. I compare the friction electrostatic
machine (Plate 160) to my sketch of the foot

        with the oscillating
flywheel in place of the anklebone set in motion by the

---

39 Pictorial Encyclopedia

leg's forward thrust and a little protruding bevel on the flat outer side of the flywheel connected 1) to a wire worn invisibly under the clothes attached to the back of the belt and 2) by a small metal rod attached to the tip of the foot which lifts with each step to prevent the foot from dragging on the carpet.

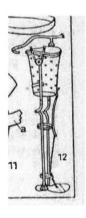

Eat

　　　　　　　To prevent the foot from
dragging on the carpet. *Nu* eat you might not have a
meal tomorrow Stern she says let me stroke

　　　　　　　your hair back on my
forehead lays my head into her right hand on her lap
and with her left fingers spread out drives them
through my hair forces my head slightly back by the
force of her stroking lifts the back of my head toward
the driving hand I hear the rhythm of her drawing on
her *Stella* above me I hear it like water in a dream of
wind and a space opens among trees and I am on a
forest path lined with blooming fuchsias the light a
gloaming eat she says you might

　　　　　　　not have a meal
tomorrow drops my head steps to the window.

Sleep

                    Steps to the window
lights another *Stella* extinguishes the match with a
sudden fluttering and looks surprised at the black
match head which emits a twittering as from birds in a
tree in front of a window in Berlin I can hear she says
⟨ birds like small dishes rattling in a cupboard then the
match ⟩

                    head falls silent and
stands in her hand slightly vibrating Stern it doesn't
matter she looks at me with eyes dark as falling how it
tastes *Hauptsache es füllt den Magen* main thing it fills
the stomach sleep you might

                    not have a bed tomorrow.

133

Achnowledgments

I am grateful to a number of people who have supported me in the writing of *Miriam's Book*. Tess Gallagher's enthusiastic advocacy was absolutely vital to my confidence in this work, and I am deeply indebted to her. Charles Borkhuis' insightful several readings were essential, and so were Kathleen Page's generous comments. G.C. Waldrep was an early supporter of this poem and I thank him very much. Many thanks also to Cynthia Hogue for her generosity. I am very grateful to Marc Estrin for his quick and decisive resolve to publish this book, and for his careful editorial comments. Thanks also to Donna Bister who saw this book with great care through production, to Delia Robinson for the gorgeous painting on the cover, and to Phoebe West for the excellent design of the book cover. My deepest gratitude goes to my wife Saundra Kay Morris, who never wavered in her encouragement when I disappeared for days in a fever of writing and who is always my best reader.

Some lines from "Bird" appeared in a different context in *The Georgia Review* (Winter 2015). An early and shorter prose version of *Miriam's Book* was among the Honorable Mentions at *Glimmer Train* (Dec. 2015). I am grateful to Christoph Volaucnik, Stadtarchiv Feldkirch, for granting permission to reproduce the image of the bombed *Reservelazaret Antoniushaus* and to Hansjörg Jäger for helping me to locate the owner of those copyrights. Thanks also to Hans Peter Treichler for providing information regarding the image of the Maggi factory and to Emanuel Saunders who facilitated the reprinting of the photo of the woman on the bench from the Photo Archives at Yad Vashem.

About the Author

Harold Schweizer's poems have appeared in *American Poetry Review, Cincinnati Review, Georgia Review, Kenyon Review, Missouri Review* (online), *Narrative, New Orleans Review, Pleiades, Ploughshares, Poetry International* and other venues. He is the author of *The Book of Stones and Angels* (poems), as well as *On Waiting, Rarity and the Poetic: The Gesture of Small Flowers,* and *Suffering and the Remedy of Art* among many other prose publications. He is Professor of English at Bucknell University.

For more information, visit www.haroldschweizer.com

Fomite

A fomite is a medium capable of transmitting infectious organisms from one individual to another.

"The activity of art is based on the capacity of people to be infected by the feelings of others." Tolstoy, *What Is Art?*

Writing a review on Amazon, Good Reads, Shelfari, Library Thing or other social media sites for readers will help the progress of independent publishing. To submit a review, go to the book page on any of the sites and follow the links for reviews. Books from independent presses rely on reader to reader communications.

For more information or to order any of our books, visit http://www.fomitepress.com/FOMITE/Our_Books.html

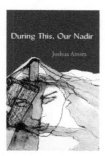

During This, Our Nadir
Joshua Amses

In the Wake of Our Vows
Neil Connelly

Hyde
Marc Estrin

Off to the Next Wherever
John Micahel Flynn

*Snake in the Spine,
Wolf in the Heart*
Barry Goldensohn

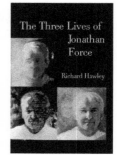

*The Three Lives
of Jonathan Force*
Richard Hawley

Fomite

Father Figure
Lamar Herrin

The Fall of Athens
Gail Holst-Warhaft

A Rising Tide of People
Swept Away
Scott Archer Jones

Shadowboxing
With Bukowski
Darrell Kastin

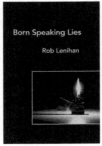

Born Speaking Lies
Rob Lenihan

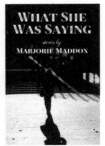

What She Was Saying
Marjorie Maddox

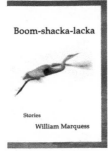

Boom-shacka-lacka
Willliam Marquess

Artsy-Fartsy
dug Nap

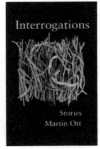

Interrogations
Martin Ott

Fomite

Connecting the Dots to Shangrila
Joseph D. Reich

Shirtwaist
Delia Bell Robinson

Isles of the Blind
Robert Rosenberg

What We Do For Love
Ron Savage

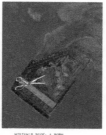

Miriam's Book: A Poem
Harold Schweizer

We
Peter Schumann

Faust 3
Peter Schumann

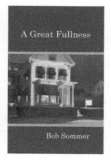

A Great Fullness
Bob Sommer

To Join the Lost
Seth Steinzor

Fomite

Among the Lost
Seth Steinzor

A Day in the Life
Tom Walker

Dispatches from Everest
Claire Zoghb

More Titles from Fomite...

Joshua Amses — *Raven or Crow*

Joshua Amses — *The Moment Before an Injury*

Jaysinh Birjepatel — *The Good Muslim of Jackson Heights*

Jaysinh Birjepatel — *Nothing Beside Remains*

Antonello Borra — *Alfabestiario*

Antonello Borra — *AlphaBetaBestiaro*

Jay Boyer — *Flight*

Micheal Breiner — *the way none of this happened*

David Brizer — *Victor Rand*

Paula Closson Buck —*Summer on the Cold War Planet*

Michael Cocchiarale — *Still Time*

James Connolly — *Picking Up the Bodies*

Greg Delanty — *Loosestrife*

Fomite

Catherine Zobal Dent — *Unfinished Stories of Girls*

Mason Drukman — *Drawing on Life*

J. C. Ellefson—*Foreign Tales of Exemplum and Woe*

Zdravka Evtimova—*Carts and Other Stories*

Zdravka Evtimova — *Sinfonia Bulgarica*

Anna Faktorovich — *Improvisational Arguments*

Daniel Forbes—*Derail This Train Wreck*

Derek Furr — *Semitones*

Derek Furr — *Suite for Three Voices*

Elizabeth Genovise — *Where There Are Two or More*

Stephen Goldberg — *Screwed and Other Plays*

Barry Goldensohn — *The Hundred Yard Dash Man*

Barry Goldensohn — *The Listener Aspires to the Condition of Music*

R. L. Green When — *You Remember Deir Yassin*

Greg Guma — *Dons of Time*

Andrei Guriuanu — *Body of Work*

Ron Jacobs — *All the Sinners Saints*

Ron Jacobs — *Short Order Frame Up*

Ron Jacobs — *The Co-conspirator's Tale*

Zeke Jarvis — *In A Family Way*

Maggie Kast — *A Free Unsullied Land*

Coleen Kearon — *Feminist on Fire*

Jan Englis Leary — *Thicker Than Blood*

Roger Leboitz — *A Guide to the Western Slopes and the Outlying Area*

Diane Lefer — *Confessions of a Carnivore*

Fomite

Kate MaGill — *Roadworthy Creature, Roadworthy Craft*

Tony Magistrale — *Entanglements*

Michele Markarian — *Unborn Children of America*

Gary Miller — *Museum of the Americas*

Ilan Mochari — *Zinsky the Obscure*

Jennifer Anne Moses — *Visiting Hours*

Sherry Olson — *Four-Way Stop*

Andy Potok — *My Father's Keeper*

Janice Miller Potter — *Meanwell*

Jack Pulaski — *Love's Labours*

Charles Rafferty — *Saturday Night at Magellan's*

Joseph D. Reich — *The Hole That Runs Through Utopia*

Joseph D. Reich — *The Housing Market*

Joseph D. Reich — *The Derivation of Cowboys and Indians*

Kathryn Roberts — *Companion Plants*

David Schein — *My Murder and Other Local News*

Peter Schumann — *Planet Kasper, Volumes One and Two*

Peter Schumann — *Bread & Sentences*

Fred Skolnik — *Rafi's World*

Lynn Sloan — *Principles of Navigation*

L.E. Smith — *The Consequence of Gesture*

L.E. Smith — *Views Cost Extra*

L.E. Smith — *Travers' Inferno*

Scott T. Starbuck — *Industrial Oz*

Susan Thomas — *The Empty Notebook Interrogates Itself*

Fomite

Susan Thomas — *Among Angelic Orders*

Tom Walker — *Signed Confessions*

Sharon Webster — *Everyone Lives Here*

Susan V. Weiss—*My God, What Have We Done?*

Tony Whedon — *The Tres Riches Heures*

Tony Whedon — *The Falkland Quartet*

Peter M. Wheelwright — *As It Is On Earth*

Suzie Wizowaty — *The Return of Jason Green*

Silas Dent Zobal — *The Inconvenience of the Wings*